Contents

BIRMINGHAM CITY UNIVERSITY
Book no. 3447014X
Subject n. 823 |Kip
LIBRARY

Introduction

It was a very young brown child – with big eyes and no clothes. He was not afraid. He looked up at Father Wolf and laughed.
   'Is that a man's cub?' said Mother Wolf. 'Show me. Bring it here.'

And so a family of wolves take the little boy into their home. The child learns and plays with the other cubs. But can Mowgli really live in the jungle? Will the wolves want him in their Pack? And will the dangerous tiger Shere Khan catch him?

Rudyard Kipling, the writer of these stories, was born in Bombay in India in 1865. His father sent him to school in England, but he went back to India at the age of seventeen. He stayed there for seven years, and worked for English-language newspapers. At this time he began to write short stories. He also wrote longer stories – *Kim* (1901), about a British boy in India, is perhaps his best book.

The Jungle Book came out in 1894. Readers of all ages loved it then, and they love it now. They also love Kipling's *Just So Stories* (1902). Kipling knew about animals, but in *Just So Stories* and in *The Jungle Book* the animals are really people. In *The Jungle Book* dangerous snakes say, 'Take him away. He is too excited. He will hurt our babies. Take him away.' Mothers are mothers – people or animals.

Rudyard Kipling's life ended in 1936 in a beautiful old house in Sussex in England.

Animals in this Story

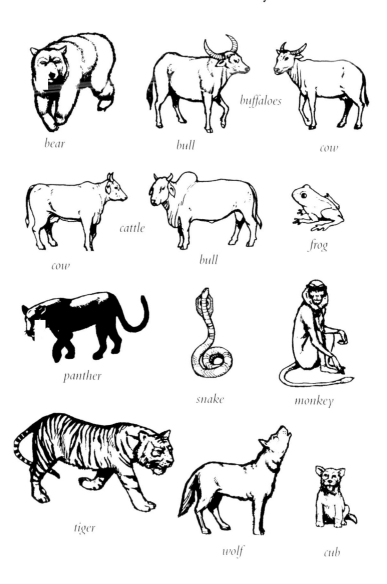

bear

buffaloes

bull

cow

cattle

cow

bull

frog

panther

snake

monkey

tiger

wolf

cub

Chapter 1   The Man-Cub

At seven o'clock on a hot evening in the Seeonee mountains, Father Wolf woke up in his cave. He looked at Mother Wolf and their four cubs in the moonlight.

'It's time to go hunting again,' said Father Wolf.

He was nearly ready when a little animal arrived at the cave.

'Good hunting, Great Wolf,' the little animal said. 'And I hope your fine children will have strong white teeth. I hope they will always remember other hungry animals.'

It was Tabaqui, the jungle dog. The wolves in India don't like Tabaqui. He makes trouble. He goes to the houses of men and looks for food. Father Wolf looked at the dog. Tabaqui wanted to make trouble now.

'Shere Khan is changing his hunting grounds,' Tabaqui said. 'He is going to hunt in these mountains.'

Shere Khan was a great tiger. He lived near the Waingunga River, thirty kilometres away.

'He can't do that!' Father Wolf said angrily. 'By the Law of the Jungle he can't change his hunting grounds. He has to tell us first. The animals will run away. And I – I have to kill for two of us, these days.'

'Shere Khan has one bad foot,' said Mother Wolf quietly. 'So they call him Lungri. He can't run very fast, so he kills the villagers' cows. Now the villagers of the Waingunga are angry with him, and he will make *our* villagers angry. They will bring fire, and that will be dangerous for us and our children.'

'You can hear him now,' said Tabaqui.

Father Wolf listened. A long way below the cave, he heard the angry cry of a hungry tiger.

'Stupid!' said Father Wolf. 'Why is he making that noise

before he hunts? The animals here are different from the fat cows in Waingunga.'

'Quiet!' said Mother Wolf. 'He isn't hunting animals tonight. He's hunting Man.'

'Man!' said Father Wolf. 'Ugh! Can't he catch a frog?'

By the Law of the Jungle, no animal can kill and eat Man. When they do, men come quickly with guns. Then they make a great noise. That is bad for everybody in the jungle. But it is also wrong because Man can't fight well. And the animals say that man-eaters become ill. Then they lose their teeth.

Suddenly there was a cry from Shere Khan – but a strange sound for a tiger. Father Wolf ran out of the cave and listened. Shere Khan screamed again from somewhere in the jungle.

'Stupid tiger,' said Father Wolf. 'Of course you hurt your feet when you jump on a woodcutter's fire.'

'Something is coming up the mountain,' said Mother Wolf. 'Be ready.'

There was a sound near the cave. Father Wolf went down on his back legs. He was ready to jump, but stopped suddenly.

'Man!' he cried. 'A man's cub. Look!'

It was a very young brown child – with big eyes and no clothes. He was not afraid. He looked up at Father Wolf and laughed.

'Is that a man's cub?' said Mother Wolf. 'Show me. Bring it here.'

A wolf doesn't hurt his cubs when he carries them. Father Wolf took the child in his teeth and put him down with the wolf cubs.

'He's very small – and very brave,' said Mother Wolf quietly. The child pushed through the cubs to Mother Wolf. 'Aha! He is taking his milk with the other cubs.'

Then something moved across the light of the moon: it was Shere Khan. Tabaqui, behind him, was excited: 'Sir, sir, it went in here!' he cried.

Father Wolf spoke quietly, but his eyes were angry.

'What do you want?' he asked Shere Khan.

'I want my food. A man-cub came here. I can see no father or mother. Give it to me.'

Shere Khan was very angry because his feet hurt. Father Wolf knew this. But the mouth of the cave was too small, and the tiger could not come in.

Father Wolf said: 'We Wolves follow the Leader of the Pack, and not a stupid tiger. The man-cub is ours.'

'*Yours?*' the tiger roared. 'What do you mean? I, Shere Khan, am speaking to you!'

Mother Wolf left the cubs and went to the tiger. 'And I, Raksha, am answering you!' she said. 'The man-cub is mine, Lungri – mine. Nobody will kill him. He will live. He will run with the Pack, and hunt with the Pack. And in the end, you hunter of little cubs – frog-eater – fish-killer, he will hunt you! Now go!'

Mother Wolf's other name was Raksha, the Dangerous One. Shere Khan moved back from the mouth of the cave. And when he was away from that dangerous place, he roared: 'We'll see. The Pack will listen to me. They will not want to look after man-cubs. The cub is mine, and I will have him between my teeth in the end!'

Mother Wolf went back to the cubs. Father Wolf said to her, 'Shere Khan is right about one thing. We will have to show the cub to the Pack. Do you want him to stay with us?'

'Stay with us?' she cried. 'He came with no clothes, at night and very hungry, but he was not afraid! He pushed my cubs out of his way. And big bad Lungri wanted to kill him, and run away to the Waingunga. Then the village men will come with guns and hunt us everywhere in these mountains. Stay with us? Of course he will stay with us. One day Mowgli – I'll call him Mowgli, the Frog – will hunt Shere Khan.'

'I will have him between my teeth in the end!'

'But what will our Pack say?' said Father Wolf.

The Law of the Jungle says: When cubs can stand on their feet, the father has to bring them in front of the Pack. The other wolves have to see them and know them. After that, the Pack will look after the cubs, and nobody can hurt them.

◆

Father Wolf took his cubs and Mowgli and Mother Wolf to the meeting place on the top of the mountain. The Leader of the Pack at that time was Akela, the great grey wolf. From his high place, Akela looked down at about forty wolves. The cubs played in the centre.

A father or mother pushed a cub into the open place below Akela. Then the Leader of the Pack called, 'You know the Law. Look well, Wolves! Look well!'

The wolves looked at cub after cub. Sometimes one of the older wolves looked carefully at a cub, and then went quietly back to his place.

When it was time, Father Wolf pushed 'Mowgli the Frog' into the open place. The child sat there. He laughed and played happily.

Akela never moved his head. He called again, 'Look well, Wolves! Look well!'

A loud noise came from behind the wolves – it was Shere Khan. He roared loudly, 'The cub is mine. Give him to me. Why do you want a man's cub?'

Akela did not move his ears. He said, 'Look well, brave Wolves! Don't listen to Shere Khan. Look well!'

Most of the wolves shut their ears to the tiger. But one young wolf said, 'But why do we want a man's cub?'

The Law of the Jungle says: When a wolf doesn't want a new cub in the Pack, two other wolves have to speak for it. They cannot be its father and mother.

'Who is going to speak for this cub?' said Akela.

There was no answer, and Mother Wolf got ready for a fight.

One other animal, not a wolf, can speak at Pack meetings. Baloo, the sleepy brown bear, teaches the wolf-cubs the Law of the Jungle, and he can go everywhere. Old Baloo stood up on his back legs and spoke.

'The man-cub?' he said. 'I will speak for the man-cub. A man-cub hurts nobody. Why can he not run with the Pack? I, Baloo, will teach him.'

'Is there another speaker?' asked Akela. 'Baloo is the teacher of our young cubs. Will any other animal speak for the man-cub?'

Something moved. It was Bagheera, the Black Panther. Everybody knew Bagheera, and nobody wanted to fight with him. He was quicker than Tabaqui, braver than other animals, and very dangerous. But he spoke as quietly as a summer night.

'Akela and all you brave wolves,' he said quietly, 'you didn't ask me to your meeting. But the Law of the Jungle says: " When the Pack does not want a cub, another animal can buy that cub." Am I right?'

'Right!' said the young wolves. They were always hungry. 'Listen to Bagheera. We can sell the cub. It is the Law. Speak, Bagheera.'

The Black Panther said, 'There is a dead buffalo – a fat one – nearly a kilometre from here. I will give you that buffalo. But the cub has to live and run with the Pack.'

There was a lot of noise: 'Why not? He will die in the cold months. Or he will die in the hot months. How can a funny frog hurt us? He can run with the Pack. Where is the buffalo, Bagheera?'

And then they heard Akela: 'Look well, Wolves! Look well!'

Mowgli didn't stop his game when the wolves looked at him. Then they all went down the mountain for the dead bull. Only Akela, Bagheera, Baloo and Mowgli's wolves stayed at the top of the mountain. Shere Khan roared somewhere in the night. He was very angry about the man–cub.

'I will give you that buffalo. But the cub has to live and run with the Pack.'

'We did the right thing,' said Akela. 'Men and their cubs know a lot of things. Perhaps he will help us one day.'

'Yes,' said Bagheera, 'because the Pack will not always have a good leader.'

'Take him away,' Akela said to Father Wolf. 'Teach him to be a brave Wolf.'

So Mowgli became a cub in the Seeonee Wolf Pack.

Chapter 2   The Red Flower

In the next ten or eleven years, Mowgli had wonderful times with the wolves. He grew up with the cubs, and Father Wolf taught him well. He learned to live in the jungle. He understood every sound, every change in the wind, every note of a bird's song, every jump of a little fish in the water.

At other times, Mowgli sat in the sun and slept. Then he ate, and slept again. When he was dirty or hot, he swam in the small jungle rivers. He climbed trees with Bagheera.

He took his place at Pack meetings. The wolves were afraid of him when he looked into their eyes. They turned away. But he helped them when they cut their feet in the jungle.

Sometimes Mowgli went down from the mountains at night. He watched the villagers in their little houses. But men were dangerous – he knew that. Sometimes Bagheera showed him hunters in the jungle.

He grew strong and brave. 'Be careful of Shere Khan,' Mother Wolf told him. 'One day, you will have to kill him.' But Mowgli didn't remember that lesson, because he was only a boy, and not a young wolf.

Akela was now older and weaker, so Shere Khan was often near Mowgli in the jungle. The tiger wanted to make friends with the younger wolves. They followed him because he sometimes left food for them. Akela didn't like it, but he was too old. He couldn't stop them.

Shere Khan said, 'Why do you fine young hunters stay in a Pack with a man-cub and an old wolf for a leader? They say that you can't look into the man-cub's eyes.' So the young wolves were angry and hated Mowgli.

Bagheera heard about this and spoke to Mowgli.

Mowgli laughed and said, 'But I have the Pack, and I have you. And Baloo will always fight for me. I am not afraid.'

'Open your eyes, Little Brother. Shere Khan is not dangerous to you in the jungle. But remember – Akela is old now. When he can't kill, he will not be the leader. And the older wolves are becoming weak. The young wolves listen to Shere Khan. They do not want a man-cub in the Pack.'

Mowgli said, 'I always follow the Law of the Jungle. And I help every wolf in the Pack. They are my brothers!'

'Brothers? They want to kill you.'

'But why? Why do they want to kill me?'

'Look at me,' said Bagheera. And Mowgli looked into his eyes. The big panther turned his head away. 'Because they have to turn away,' he said. 'They hate you because their eyes cannot meet yours. Because – yes – because you are a man.'

'I did not know that,' said Mowgli.

'You have to know that,' his friend said. 'Listen. When Akela cannot kill, the Pack will fight him. They will fight you too. First they will have a meeting on top of the mountain, and then – and then – Ah! I know the answer! You will have to go down to the village at the foot of the mountain, and find some Red Flower. Then, when the time comes, you will have a stronger friend than Baloo or me or the older wolves. Get the Red Flower.'

Bagheera meant fire. He called it the Red Flower because he

was afraid of it. Every animal was afraid of it.

'The Red Flower?' said Mowgli. 'It lives outside their houses in little pots. I will get some.'

He went down to the little river at the foot of the mountain. And there he stopped, because he heard the sound of the Pack and a bigger animal. There was a hunt, his ears told him. He heard a fight. Then the young wolves cried: 'Akela! Akela! You are strong! Kill him, Akela!'

Mowgli listened carefully. His ears told him everything. Akela went in without the Pack and fought the big animal. But Akela's teeth were old and weak and he fell.

Mowgli didn't wait. He went into the village and looked through a window. He saw a child there. The child had some fire in a pot and brought it outside. Mowgli took the fire pot from the child.

◆

The next day, Mowgli learned about the fire pot.

In the evening, Tabaqui came. 'You have to go to the top of the mountain,' he said. But Mowgli laughed, and Tabaqui ran away, afraid.

But Mowgli did go to the top of the mountain.

Akela was not on the highest place; he was too weak.

'Another wolf will now become the Leader of the Pack,' Mowgli thought.

Shere Khan, with his young wolf friends, walked openly on the top of the mountain.

Mowgli sat down, with the fire pot between his legs, and Bagheera came to him.

Shere Khan began to speak. He was only brave because Akela was old and ill.

Mowgli jumped up. 'Brave Wolves,' he cried, 'is Shere Khan

the Leader of the Pack? Why is he here with us?'

Akela looked up. 'Brave Wolves – and you, too, dogs of Shere Khan – for many years I took you hunting. Nobody hurt you or caught you. Now I cannot kill. So you are right – you have to kill me here on the top of the mountain. Who will finish Akela? The Law of the Jungle says that you have to come one after the other.'

Nobody spoke. No wolf wanted to fight Akela.

Then Shere Khan said, 'Bah! Why are we thinking about this stupid old wolf? He is going to die. The *man-cub* is important to *me*. Brave Wolves, he was mine in the beginning. Give him to me.'

Akela spoke again. 'Mowgli ate our food. He lived with us. He helped us in the hunt. He always followed the Law of the Jungle.'

'He is a man – a man!' cried the young wolves angrily, and they moved nearer Shere Khan.

'Now your friends can do nothing more – only fight for you,' said Bagheera.

Mowgli stood up, with the fire pot in his hands.

'Listen!' he cried. 'I want to be a wolf. I want to stay with you in the Pack. But you say that I am a man. So I have to listen to you. I will not call you my brothers now. Men call you dogs, and I will call you dogs too. I have here some Red Flower. Look at it and be afraid!'

He threw the fire pot on the ground, and the fire fell out. The wolves were afraid and moved away. Mowgli put some wood on the fire and it became stronger.

'Good!' said Mowgli. 'I was right – you are dogs. I am going to leave you. I will be a man in the world of men. But first I have to speak to this animal.'

He walked to Shere Khan. The tiger looked stupidly at the fire. Bagheera followed Mowgli because he was afraid for him.

'This tiger,' Mowgli said, 'wanted to kill me here, because he is angry. He could not kill me when I was a cub. Well, men hit dogs. When you touch me, Shere Khan, I will push the Red Flower into your mouth.' He hit Shere Khan on the head with his fire-wood, and the tiger roared.

'Bah!' said Mowgli. 'Are you brave now? Go! But listen, Wolves. When I next come to the top of the mountain, I will come with Shere Khan's skin. And listen again, Wolves: You will not kill Akela. And I do not think that Shere Khan's "friends" will come here again. Now go!'

The fire was hot and strong at the end of the wood, and Mowgli hit the young wolves with it. They screamed and ran.

Only Akela, Bagheera, and perhaps ten of the older wolves stayed. Then something began to hurt Mowgli inside, and his face was wet.

'What is wrong with me?' he asked. 'Am I dying, Bagheera?'

'No, Little Brother, you are crying. Now I know you are a man. You are not a man-cub now. Do not be afraid, Mowgli. Men cry.'

So, for the first time, Mowgli cried.

'Now,' he said, 'I will go to men. But first I will say goodbye to my mother.' And he went to the cave, and he cried on Mother Wolf's coat.

Then Mowgli went down the mountain. He had to meet those strange animals, men.

Chapter 3   The Bandar-log

This is a story from the days when Baloo was Mowgli's teacher. It was before Mowgli left the Seeonee Wolf Pack.

The big old brown bear, Baloo, was happy because Mowgli learnt quickly. The man-cub had to learn more than a young wolf. The boy could climb quickly and run fast. He could swim well. So Baloo taught him the language of the jungle. Then he could call to the other animals.

He hit Shere Khan on the head with his fire-wood . . .

'Say the words for the birds,' Baloo told him.

The answer was a high bird call.

'Now for the snakes,' said Baloo.

'We are brothers, you and I,' said Mowgli, with the *hiss* of a snake.

'Now he doesn't have to be afraid of anybody,' Baloo told Bagheera.

Mowgli laughed. 'I am not afraid of old Baloo!' he said. 'I will go up the trees and throw wood down at old Baloo. The Bandar-log do that. They will help me.'

'Mowgli,' said Baloo, 'you can't talk to the Bandar-log, the tree monkeys. I told you that.' His eyes were angry.

Mowgli looked at Bagheera; the panther was angry too.

'In the old days,' said Mowgli, 'the Bandar-log came down from the trees and were kind to me. I did not have any friends then.'

Baloo was really angry. 'Listen, Man-cub!' he said. 'I taught you the Law of the Jungle for every animal, but not for the Bandar-log. They have no law. Their way is not our way. They have no leaders. They remember nothing. We do not talk to the monkeys. We do not drink in the same places. We do not go to the same places. We do not hunt in the same places. Is this or is this not our first conversation about the Bandar-log?'

'It is,' said Mowgli, very quietly. He was afraid of Baloo when he was angry.

'Yes,' said Baloo. 'We do not talk about them. There are a lot of them, and they are bad, dirty animals. We do not turn round when they throw things at our heads. Remember that.'

When Baloo spoke, there were monkeys high up in the trees above their heads. They followed Baloo, Bagheera and Mowgli through the jungle very quietly, and then it was time for the midday sleep. Mowgli walked between the panther and the bear.

'I will never think about the Bandar-log again,' he told them.

Suddenly, hard, strong little hands took him and carried him up into the treetops. He could see his friends a long way down on the ground. Baloo roared loudly; Bagheera climbed angrily up into the trees.

The Bandar-log made a lot of noise and took Mowgli up to the tops of the trees. The panther could not follow them there. Then the monkeys jumped from tree to tree.

For a time, Mowgli was afraid. In some places he was thirty metres from the ground. But then he began to think. Baloo and Bagheera couldn't go as fast as the monkeys. How could they help him?

He looked down, and saw only trees. So he looked up, and saw a big bird, high in the blue sky. It was Chil. Chil saw everything in the jungle with his wonderful eyes. He came down three or four hundred metres to the treetops and saw Mowgli with the monkeys. His head turned quickly when Mowgli gave the bird call for: 'We are brothers, you and I.'

It was difficult to see the boy in the trees after that, but Chil flew to the next high place on the monkey road. The little brown face came up again.

' Watch me!' Mowgli shouted. 'And tell Baloo of the Seeonee Pack and Bagheera of the mountain top.'

' What is your name, brother?' Chil only knew about Mowgli from stories.

' Mowgli, the Frog. Man-cub, they call me.'

Chil climbed up into the sky because the monkeys could not see him there. He used his wonderful eyes. The monkeys carried Mowgli through the jungle, and the treetops moved.

◆

Down on the ground, Baloo and Bagheera talked about the problem.

' Because they live in the trees, the Bandar-log are not afraid of us,' Baloo said. ' They are only afraid of Kaa, the great snake. Kaa can climb as well as they can. He takes young monkeys in the night. Perhaps he will help us.'

Baloo and Bagheera found Kaa in the sun. He was very happy with his new skin. The beautiful new brown and yellow snake skin was ten metres long.

'Good hunting, Kaa!' cried Baloo.

'Oho, Baloo, what are you doing here? Are you looking for food? I, too, am hungry.'

'We are hunting,' said Baloo slowly. Kaa liked to do everything slowly. 'We are looking for the Bandar-log,' said Bagheera. 'Those dirty monkeys have our man-cub. Perhaps you know about him.'

Kaa said, 'I did hear something about a man-thing in a wolf pack.'

'Our man-cub is in the hands of the Bandar-log now,' said Baloo. 'They are only afraid of Kaa. And so we came to you.'

'It is very dangerous for the man-thing,' said the snake. 'Where are they?'

'We do not know,' said Baloo very sadly.

'Up! Up! Look up, Baloo of the Seeonee Pack! Look up!' Baloo looked up and saw Chil in the evening sky.

'What is it?' Baloo called.

'Mowgli is with the Bandar-log. They are taking him across the river to the monkey city.'

They all knew about the city. When men left it, hundreds of years before, the jungle took it. The monkeys often went there, but the other animals did not. They stayed away from places of men.

'It is half a night's journey,' said Bagheera.

'You and Kaa go quickly,' said Baloo. 'I will follow you as fast as I can.'

The fast panther, Bagheera, ran away. The great snake went quickly too.

Chapter 4   Kaa Goes Hunting

In the old city, the monkeys forgot about Mowgli's friends. They had the boy, and they were very happy. It was Mowgli's first visit to a city. This was very old, and the tops of the houses were open to the sky. Trees pushed through the old walls. But it was wonderful in Mowgli's eyes.

The monkeys brought him there late in the afternoon, and then they began to play in the old houses. They ran up and down the old city roads, and threw things. They drank and made the water dirty.

'Do they never sleep, these Bandar-log?' Mowgli thought. 'I want food,' he shouted at them. 'I do not know this place, so bring me food. Or I will have to hunt.'

Twenty or thirty monkeys ran for food from the jungle trees. But they started fighting on the way, and forgot about the food.

When Mowgli went near the city wall, the monkeys pulled him back.

'Do not leave us,' they said. 'We are a great people. We are the most wonderful people in the jungle.'

They took him to a building. There were no doors or windows in the building – only very old white walls. There was water round it, and it looked beautiful in the moonlight.

The open place in front of the white building was a meeting place for the monkeys. Hundreds of them came and stood round Mowgli.

'The Bandar-log are wonderful!' they shouted. 'We all know that!'

'They never sleep,' Mowgli thought. 'But perhaps I can run away when it is darker. I am very tired.'

◆

17

'Do they never sleep, these Bandar-log?' Mowgli thought.

Two good friends watched the same sky. They were outside the city, and they made a plan. Bagheera and Kaa knew the monkeys well. 'They are dangerous in large numbers. The monkeys only fight when there are a hundred monkeys and one other animal.'

'I will go round to the back of the city,' Kaa said, 'and then I will come down the mountain very fast. But–'

'I know,' said Bagheera. 'Baloo is not here, and I am sorry about that. But we have to try. When the moon starts to go down, I will climb up there. The boy is there with the monkeys.'

'Good hunting!' said Kaa. And he moved quickly away to the wall at the back of the city. That wall was the biggest and best, but the snake found a way over it. The sky began to get darker.

Mowgli suddenly heard Bagheera's quiet feet. The Black Panther ran up the mountain very fast and started hitting the monkeys. His feet were quicker than his teeth.

The monkeys near Mowgli screamed and tried to get away. But then one monkey shouted, 'There is only one here! Kill him!'

Fifty of the biggest and bravest monkeys jumped on Bagheera. He felt their teeth, hands and feet on him. Mowgli wanted to help him, but five or six big monkeys caught him. They pulled him up the wall of the building. Then they threw him down. He fell five metres to the floor inside – a long way for a boy. But Mowgli was strong, and he stayed on his feet.

'Stay there,' the monkeys shouted. 'We will kill your friend, then we will kill you.'

Mowgli quickly made the snake call. 'We are brothers, you and I,' he said, with the *hiss* of a snake. He heard snakes all round him on the floor. So he made the snake call again.

'Yesss, yesss!' said a number of snakes. 'Don't move – stay there, little brother. Your feet will hurt us. Don't move.'

Mowgli stood as quietly as he could. He tried to see between the old walls. He heard the great fight round the Black Panther – the monkeys' shouts and screams, and Bagheera's angry cries.

'Don't move – stay there, little brother. Your feet will hurt us.'

Mowgli's friend turned this way and that way. He fought under a great sea of monkeys. For the first time in many years, Bagheera had to fight for his life.

'Where's Baloo?' Mowgli thought. And then he called, 'To the water, Bagheera! Fight your way to the water! Get to the water!'

Bagheera heard him. Now he knew – Mowgli was not dead. And that helped the Black Panther. He fought his way slowly to the water.

Then, from the wall of the old city, came the sound of an angry bear. Old Baloo was there.

'Bagheera,' he shouted, 'I am here! I am climbing! I am coming as fast as I can! Wait for me! Wait for me, you dirty Bandar-log!'

Baloo got near the water – and he too went under a sea of monkeys. He began to hit them with his great arms. He threw dead monkeys to the left and to the right.

Bagheera was in the water now, and the monkeys could not follow him. They stood and shouted angrily.

Then Bagheera gave the snake call: 'We are brothers, you and I.' Where was Kaa? Did he not want to hear him?

Baloo – under his great sea of monkeys – laughed when he heard Bagheera.

But Kaa did hear, and he did not turn away. He came down the mountain fast.

Remember – Kaa was ten metres long! He angrily started to hit the monkeys round Baloo. His head cut through them. He didn't have to try a second time. He killed a lot of monkeys, and the others ran away.

'Kaa! It's Kaa!' they screamed. 'Run! Run!'

Young monkeys are afraid of Kaa. Their parents tell stories about the snake. 'What happens to bad little monkeys? Kaa comes for them! He can move through the trees without a sound. He can take away the strongest and cleverest monkey.'

No monkey could look into the great snake's eyes. When he killed the biggest, strongest monkey, that was the end.

So the monkeys screamed because they were afraid. They ran to the tops of the old walls. Baloo had to stop. His coat was stronger than Bagheera's but he had bad cuts from the monkeys' teeth.

Then Kaa opened his mouth for the first time. One long *hissssss* came from it. The monkeys on the walls and the open houses were suddenly quiet. The city and the jungle round it were quiet when they heard that angry sound.

Bagheera climbed out of the water. The screams of the monkeys started again, and they tried to climb higher up the walls.

Bagheera said, 'We have to take the man-cub and go. I cannot fight again.'

'The Bandar-log will only move when I tell them. Sssstay, Bandar-log!' Kaa said, and the city was quiet again. 'I could not come to you before, Brother,' the great snake said. 'But I think I heard your call, Bagheera.'

'Well – yes – perhaps I did call in the fight,' Bagheera answered. 'Baloo, are you hurt?'

'I think I have a hundred cuts,' Baloo said. 'Yes, I am hurt. Kaa, you helped Bagheera and me when it was very dangerous. Thank you for our lives.'

'I wanted to help. Where is the man-cub?'

'Here! I cannot climb out,' cried Mowgli.

'Take him away,' said the snakes inside. 'He is too excited. He will hurt our babies. Take him away.'

'Ha!' laughed Kaa. 'He has friends everywhere, this man-cub. Stand away from the wall, Man-cub. And be careful, snakes. I am going to break down the wall.'

Kaa looked carefully at the white wall of the building and saw a weak place in it. He pushed the place two or three times with his head. Then he hit it very hard five or six great times.

The wall fell down. Mowgli jumped out and stood between Baloo and Bagheera.

'Did they hurt you?' asked Baloo kindly.

'A little – and I am very hungry. But, oh, my brothers, they hurt you very badly.'

'Not only me,' said Bagheera, and he looked round at the dead monkeys. 'But here is Kaa. He won the fight for us. Thank him for your life, Mowgli.'

The great snake's head moved from left to right, nearly half a metre over Mowgli's little head.

'So this is the man-cub?' Kaa said. 'He is not very different from the Bandar-log. Be careful, Man-cub. I will think you are a monkey one evening.'

'We are brothers, you and I,' Mowgli answered. 'Thank you. When I kill, it will be yours.' He said the right thing.

'Thank you, little brother,' said Kaa. Mowgli didn't hear his quiet laugh. 'And what do you kill, brave hunter?'

'I do not kill anything – I am too young. But I help with the hunt. And I have these hands. One day I will use them for you – and for Bagheera and Baloo. Good hunting!'

'Fine words,' said Baloo, because Mowgli said thank you well.

'You are brave, little brother,' said Kaa, 'and you say the right things. But now go away with your friends and sleep. Bad things are going to happen here.'

The moon was now half-way down behind the mountains. The monkeys on the walls made no sound. Baloo went down to the water for a drink. Bagheera began to move away. Then Kaa went quietly to the open place near the water. His mouth shut with a loud hard sound, and the monkeys looked at him.

'The moon is going down,' he said. 'Can you see?'

The monkeys were really afraid now. 'Yes, great Kaa, we can see.'

'Good. Now the dance begins – the Night Dance of Kaa. Sit quietly and watch.'

He began to do a strange snake-dance. He moved this way and that. He never went fast but he never stopped.

Baloo and Bagheera did not move. Mowgli looked and tried to understand.

'Bandar-log,' said Kaa. 'Can you move without my word? Ssspeak!' Kaa's eyes never left them.

'Without your word we cannot move a hand or a foot, great Kaa!'

'Good! Come nearer!'

The monkeys went nearer. They had to move. Baloo and Bagheera went nearer too.

'Again!' And they all moved again.

Mowgli put his hands on Baloo and Bagheera, and the two animals jumped.

'Leave your hand on me.' Bagheera spoke very quietly. 'Leave it on me, or I will go to Kaa. I have to go to Kaa!'

'He is only dancing,' said Mowgli. 'Come away.' And the three animals went into the jungle.

Baloo was better when he was under the great trees again. 'I will not ask for Kaa's help again,' he said.

'We nearly walked into his mouth,' Bagheera said.

'A lot of monkeys will walk in there before the sun comes up,' said Baloo. 'He will have good hunting.'

Mowgli didn't understand. 'What happened to the monkeys? The big snake only did a stupid dance! And did you see his nose? Ha, ha, ha!'

'Mowgli,' said Bagheera angrily, 'he broke his nose for you. And my ears and back hurt, and Baloo's head hurts.'

'Yes,' said Baloo, 'but we have the man-cub again.'

'Yes. But we did no hunting and I, the Black Panther, had to call Kaa. Because you, Man-cub, talked to the Bandar-log.'

'I know,' said Mowgli. 'I am really sorry.'

'Hm! What does the Law of the Jungle say, Baloo?'

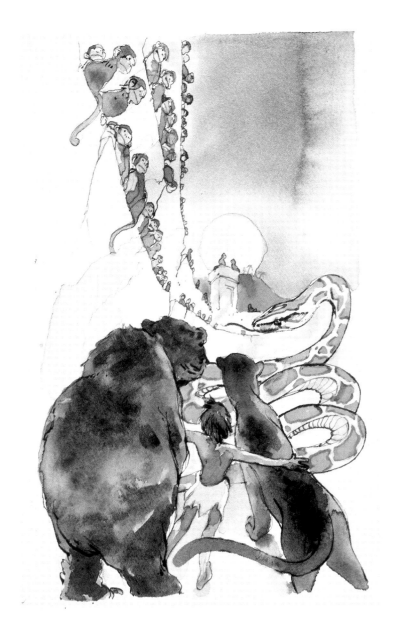

Kaa's eyes never left them.

'It says: "When you are sorry, that does not pay for the bad things." But remember, Bagheera, he is very small.'

'I will remember. But he was wrong, and we will have to hit him. Do you want to say anything, Mowgli?'

'Nothing. I was wrong. They hurt you and Baloo. Hit me!'

Bagheera hit him 'lightly'. But he was a panther, and it really hurt the seven-year-old boy. Mowgli stood up again and said nothing.

'Now,' said Bagheera, 'jump on my back, little brother, and we will go home.'

Chapter 5   In the Land of Men

Now we go back to the end of the first story, when Mowgli left the wolf cave after the fight on the mountain top. He didn't stop at the first village. It was too near the jungle, and some animals there hated him. So he ran for thirty kilometres or more.

The open country in front of him had no mountains, but there were dry river beds across it. When the rains came, the water ran fast through them. The water cut deep into the ground and the banks between the river and the land were high. There was a small village, and then the open country met the jungle. There were cattle and buffaloes there, with some small boys.

When the small boys saw Mowgli, they ran away. People came from the village and looked at Mowgli. They talked and shouted.

Then a fat man arrived. 'Do not be afraid,' he said to the villagers. 'Look at his arms and legs.' When Mowgli played with the cubs, their teeth left white cuts on his skin. 'Wolves' teeth did that. He is a wolf-child from the jungle.'

'Ah!' a woman said. 'Wolves' teeth? That is very sad! Messua, he has the face of your little boy before the tiger took him.'

A kind woman came to Mowgli. 'Yes,' she said. 'He has got my boy's face.'

'Take him to your house, Messua,' the fat man said. 'Perhaps he is your son. Perhaps he is not. But the jungle took your boy, and this child is from the jungle.'

The kind woman spoke to Mowgli. He didn't understand her words, but she showed him the way. He followed her. They went into her house, and she gave him milk and bread. Then she put her hand on his head and looked into his eyes.

'Are you my son?' she asked. 'Are you Nathoo? Nathoo?'

Mowgli's face showed nothing.

'No,' she said sadly. 'But you will be my son now.'

Mowgli looked round the inside of her house.

'How can I be a man?' he thought. 'I do not understand their talk. I am as stupid here as a man in the jungle. I will have to learn their language.'

Mowgli listened carefully to Messua. When she said a word, he repeated the sounds of that word. Before night, he knew the words for things in the house.

When night came, Mowgli went out. He couldn't sleep in the house. Messua didn't stop him. He couldn't sleep in a bed – she knew that.

Mowgli found a good place outside, but he couldn't sleep. Then a wet nose touched him. It was Grey Brother, Mother Wolf's oldest cub.

'Pooh!' said Grey Brother. 'You are a man now. But listen, Little Brother. Shere Khan is away. He will come back when he has a new coat. The Red Flower really hurt him. But when he comes back, he will kill you. He says that he will throw you in the Waingunga River.'

'Remember *my* words,' said Mowgli. 'I will take Shere Khan's skin to the mountain top. I am tired tonight – very tired with this new life. But come again, Grey Brother. Come often, and tell me about the Seeonee mountains and the jungle.'

'Remember, Little Brother, you are a wolf. Will men change you?'

'Never. I love you and our cave. But I will also remember the other wolves. They did not want me in the Pack.'

◆

Mowgli worked hard and he learned the words and the ways of men.

In the evenings, he listened to the old men. They sat under a great tree in the village and told stories – wonderful stories. Old Buldeo, the village hunter, told the best stories. He sat with his old gun on his legs and told stories about the animals in the jungle. But they were only stories. Mowgli tried not to laugh.

But in the end the village leader – the fat man – saw Mowgli's smile. The story that evening was about a tiger with a bad foot. The great tiger carried away Messua's son.

'The big tiger with the bad foot is afraid of nothing,' Buldeo said, 'because it is a ghost. The ghost-tiger is the bravest tiger in India.'

'That boy,' said the fat leader, 'has to do some work. He can look after the village buffaloes. He will take them out in the morning. He will stay with them all day. And he will bring them back to the village in the evening. He can start tomorrow.'

So the next day, Mowgli went out in the early morning. He sat on the back of Rama, the biggest buffalo.

'Leave the cattle here,' he said to the village boys, when they were about a kilometre from the village. 'I am taking the buffaloes nearer to the jungle.'

He found the place. There the Waingunga River came out of the jungle. Mowgli got down from Rama's back and ran to some big trees.

'Ah!' said Grey Brother. 'You are here! Shere Khan waited near the village, but now he is hunting again. He will come back.'

'Good,' said Mowgli. 'Will you, or another brother, sit here when he comes back? Then I will see you when I leave the village.'

Weeks later, Mowgli saw Grey Brother at the same place.

'Shere Khan came over the mountains last night with Tabaqui,' said Grey Brother.

'Oh,' said Mowgli. 'I am not afraid of Shere Khan, but with Tabaqui too—'

'Tabaqui will not help him. I met Tabaqui this morning. Before I broke his back, he told me everything. Shere Khan is going to wait for you when you go back to the village tonight. He is waiting now in the big dry river bed.'

Mowgli stood and thought. 'Did he eat first?'

'Yes.'

'Stupid tiger!' said Mowgli. 'With food inside him, he cannot climb up the banks of the river. I can take the herd through the jungle to a place on the river. Then they will run up the river. When they see the tiger, they will be very angry. They will run at him and kill him. But we have to stop him when he runs away from them. Brother, can you help me?'

'With my friend, I can.'

Mowgli saw a great grey head. He knew that head well, and loved it.

'Akela! Thank you!' said Mowgli. 'Thank you! I want these buffaloes in two herds, Akela – the cows and their babies here, and the bulls there.'

The two wolves ran in and out of the herd, this way and that way. And quickly there were two herds.

Mowgli jumped on to Rama's back. 'Take the bulls through the jungle to the river, Akela. And you, Grey Brother, stay with the cows. Then take them to the other end of the river.'

'A long way?' Grey Brother asked.

'To a place with high banks,' Mowgli called. 'Stay there, and wait for us. We will come down the river to you.'

Grey Brother sat in front of the cows, and Akela took the bulls away. After a time he stopped, and Mowgli called quietly to the bulls. They were ready.

The two wolves ran in and out of the herd, this way and that way.

Chapter 6 Tiger!

'We have to tell the buffaloes about Shere Khan, Akela,' Mowgli said. 'They have to know before we go. And I want to tell Shere Khan about us. We have got him.'

He put his hands to his mouth and shouted down the river. The angry roar of a sleepy tiger came back: 'Who is it?'

'It is Mowgli. It is time now. You are coming back with me to the mountain top! Now! Bring them down, Akela! Quickly, Rama, down!'

Akela gave the great hunting call of the wolf, and the herd started. The bulls ran into the dry river, faster and faster. Rama saw Shere Khan and called loudly to the other bulls.

'Ha!' shouted Mowgli on his back. 'Ha! Now you know!' And the herd knew. Nothing can stop an angry herd of buffalo bulls. No tiger can stop them.

Shere Khan heard them. He started to look for a way out of the river. But the walls were too high. He ran. A call from the cows at the end of the river answered the bulls' call. Shere Khan turned.

Rama's feet hit something!

Then the bulls met the cows. For a time there was a dangerous sea of buffaloes. But, with the help of Akela and Grey Brother, Mowgli took them out of the river. The bulls slowly became quieter.

Shere Khan was dead.

'Brothers,' Mowgli said, 'that was a dog's end. But Shere Khan was not brave. He did not try to fight.' He went with the two wolves to the dead tiger. 'I will take his skin to the mountain top,' he said. 'Will you help me?'

With his knife, he started to cut the tiger's skin. It was hard work, but the two wolves helped.

After an hour, Mowgli felt a hand on him and he looked up. It was Buldeo with his gun. The wolves were not there now.

31

'What are you doing?' Buldeo said angrily. 'Why didn't you look after the herd? And do you think you can take a tiger's skin? Where did the bulls kill him? It is the tiger with a bad foot, too. I can get a hundred pounds for his skin. Leave it with me, and perhaps I will give you a pound or two.'

He started to pull Mowgli away from Shere Khan.

'Akela,' said Mowgli, 'the old man is making trouble for me.'

Buldeo was suddenly on the ground. A great grey wolf stood over him.

He didn't move. 'This is not a boy,' he thought. 'What strange man-animal is he?' Afraid, he said to Mowgli, 'Great Leader! Can I get up and go away? Or will your great grey wolf kill me?'

'Go – and do not be afraid. But never stop my hunting again. I waited a long time for this tiger with the bad foot. The old man can go, Akela.'

Buldeo ran away to the village. When he got there, he told a wonderful story of the strange Mowgli and his coversations with grey ghost-wolves.

Mowgli finished his work. It was evening when he and the wolves pulled off Shere Khan's great skin.

'Now I will have to take the buffaloes home. Help me, brothers.'

It was nearly dark when they arrived at the first houses in the village. Mowgli saw lights and heard village noises.

'Shere Khan is dead, and they are happy,' he thought.

But suddenly the villagers started to throw things at him. They shouted: 'Wolf-child! Jungle-animal! Bad monkey! Go away! Go away quickly! Kill him, Buldeo, kill him!'

The hunter's old gun make a sudden loud noise, and a scream came from an angry young buffalo.

'Now what is he doing?' shouted the villagers. 'He turned your gun and you hit your buffalo, Buldeo.'

'Your brothers are not different from the Pack,' said Akela quietly. 'I think they want you to go.'

Buldeo was suddenly on the ground. A great grey wolf stood over him.

'Again? The wolves did not want me because I was a man. Now men do not want me because I am a wolf.'

A woman – Messua – ran across to the herd.

'Oh, my son, my son! They say that you are a strange monkey. They say that you can change into other animals. I know they are wrong. But go, or they will kill you. Buldeo says you do bad things. But you killed a tiger, and that tiger took my Nathoo.'

'Come back, Messua!' they shouted. 'Come back, or we will kill you too.'

Mowgli laughed – a short laugh, because something hit him in the mouth.

'Go back to them, Messua,' he said. 'They tell those stupid stories under the big tree in the evenings. But yes, I killed the tiger for your son. Run, Messua! I am going to send the herd into the village. Goodbye!'

Akela and Grey Brother made a sound, and the herd ran into the village. People ran to the right and to the left.

'Goodbye, Men,' Mowgli shouted. 'You will not see me again.'

He turned and walked away with Akela and Grey Brother. He looked up at the night sky, and he was happy.

'We will take Shere Khan's coat and leave. We will not hurt the village, because Messua was kind to me.'

When the moon came up, the villagers saw Mowgli with the two wolves. Mowgli had something on his head. The wolves and the man-cub ran and ran, away from the village. And Messua cried.

Buldeo told his story to the other men. Akela stood up on his back legs, Buldeo said, and used the words of men.

◆

The moon was nearly down when Mowgli and the two wolves came to the mountain-top. They stopped at Mother Wolf's cave.

'They threw me out of the Man Pack, Mother,' shouted Mowgli. 'But I am bringing you the skin of Shere Khan.'

Mother Wolf walked slowly – her legs were old now – to the mouth of the cave. Her eyes were happy when she saw the tiger's skin.

'I told him that day, when he hunted you. I told him, and I was right, Little Frog. Good work.'

'Yes, good work!' It was Bagheera.

Mowgli, Bagheera and the wolves climbed up to the mountain-top, and Mowgli put the skin on the ground in Akela's old place.

Then Akela sat on Shere Khan's skin and called the old call, 'Look well, Wolves! Look well!'

But nobody heard him – there was no Pack.

'Nobody wants me – not the Man Pack and not the Wolf Pack,' said Mowgli. 'So now I will hunt alone in the jungle.'

'Not alone. We will hunt with you,' said the cubs.

So, from that day, Mowgli hunted with his brothers in the jungle.

ACTIVITIES

Chapters 1–2

Before you read

1 Find these words in your dictionary. They are all in the story.

*become   brave   cave   grow   hunt   jungle   law   leader   moon
pack   roar   scream   skin   touch   trouble*

  a Which are words for:
  – places?   – noises?

  b Use the words in these sentences.
  – The ..... says it is wrong to kill people.
  – His clothes are too small; he is ..... fast.
  – I was in the sun, and now my ..... is red.
  – I hope I will ..... a doctor after university.
  – Are you in ..... because you didn't go to school?

  c What is a word for:
  – a lot of wolves?
  – the boss?
  – put your fingers on something?
  – try to catch (or kill) an animal?

2 The Law of the Jungle is very important for the animals in this book. What do you think the law says?

After you read

3 Answer these questions.
  a Is Mowgli a wolf, a boy or a frog? What does his name mean?
  b Why does Shere Khan hate him?
  c Who speaks for Mowgli in front of the wolves?
  d Why do the young wolves hate him?
  e Why is the Red Flower important to Mowgli?

4 You are wolves. Have this conversation.
  Student A: You want Mowgli to be in the Pack.
  Student B: You think it is a bad idea.

Chapters 3–4

Before you read

5 You are going to read a story now about Mowgli when he was younger. Who were his friends, do you think? What trouble can a young man-cub get into?

After you read

6 What are these animals?
   a Bagheera   b Baloo   c the Bandar-log
   d Chil   e Kaa
7 Which animal(s):
   a have no leaders and no law?
   b has wonderful eyes?
   c is ten metres long?
   d moves quite slowly through the jungle?
8 Talk about Kaa's dance. What does he do? Why does he do it?

Chapters 5–6

Before you read

9 Earlier in the book, Mowgli left the wolves and went to the villages. What will happen to him there, do you think? Will he like it? Will he see his friends in the jungle again?
10 Find these words in your dictionary.
    alone bank ghost herd land
    a Find a place for four of the words here:
       – a ..... of cattle
       – the ..... of a river
       – the ..... of a dead animal
       – a ..... of mountains and rivers
    b If you are *alone*, who is with you?

After you read

11 Which answer is right?

    a Nathoo is:

        (i) Mowgli's brother

        (ii) a village woman

        (iii) Messua's son

    b Old Buldeo is:

        (i) a big bear

        (ii) the name of a village

        (iii) the village hunter

    c Rama is:

        (i) Shere Khan's friend

        (ii) a buffalo bull

        (iii) the village leader

    d Shere Khan dies when:

        (i) Mowgli kills him

        (ii) the buffaloes kill him

        (iii) he has to go into the water

    e At the end of the story, Mowgli lives with:

        (i) his wolf family

        (ii) the Pack

        (iii) other men

12 Does the story end happily or sadly, do you think? How is it happy? How is it sad?

Writing

13 Which person or animal do you like best in *The Jungle Book*? What do you like about them?

14 What do you know about the Law of the Jungle? What is good and bad about this law?

15 When Mowgli goes to the village, he doesn't know any 'man's talk'. What are the 10 most important words for him, do you think? Why?

16 Walt Disney made a famous film about Mowgli and his friends, with a lot of lovely music. Write a song for a new film of *The Jungle Book*.

Answers for the Activities in this book are available from your local office or alternatively write to: Penguin Readers Marketing Department, Pearson Education, Edinburgh Gate, Harlow, Essex CM20 2JE.